Holland Lop Rabbits

This publication is Copyright 2013 by EKL Publishing. All products, publications, software and services mentioned and recommended in this publication are protected by trademarks. In such instance, all trademarks & copyright belong to the respective owners.

The moral rights of the author has been asserted
British Library Cataloguing in Publication Data
A catalogue record for this book is available from the British Library
ISBN 978-1-909820-04-3

Disclaimer and Legal Notice

While every attempt has been made to verify the information shared in this publication, neither shall the author nor publisher assume any responsibility for errors, omissions, nor contrary interpretation of the subject matter herein. Any perceived slight to any specific person(s) or organisation(s) are purely unintentional. You need to do your own due diligence to determine if the content of this product is correct for you.

This book is presented solely for educational and entertainment purposes. The author and publisher are not offering it as legal, accounting, or other professional services advice. While best efforts have been used in preparing this book, the author, affiliates and publisher make no representations or warranties of any kind and assume no liabilities of any kind with respect to the accuracy or completeness of the contents and specifically disclaim any implied warranties of merchantability or fitness of use for a particular purpose. Neither shall the author nor the publisher be held liable or responsible to any person or entity with respect to any loss or incidental or consequential damages caused, or alleged to have been caused, directly or indirectly, by the information or programs contained herein. The author shall not be liable for any loss incurred as a consequence of the use and application, direct or indirectly, of any information presented in this work. This publication is designed to provide information in regard to the subject matter covered. It is the reader's responsibility to find advice before putting anything written in the book into practice.

References are provided for informational purposes only and do not constitute endorsement of any websites or other sources. Readers should be aware that the websites listed in this book may change. We have no control over the nature, content, and availability of the websites listed in this book. The inclusion of any website links does not necessarily imply a recommendation or endorse the views expressed within them. EKL Publishing takes no responsibility for, and will not be liable for, the website being temporally unavailable or being removed from the internet. The information in this book is not intended to serve as legal advice.

Holland Lop Rabbits

The Complete Owner's Guide to Holland Lop Bunnies

How to Care for your Holland Lop Pet, including
Breeding, Lifespan, Colors, Health,
Personality, Diet and Facts

Foreword

Hello and thank you for buying my book.

In this book you will find some wonderful information to help you care for your Holland Lop Rabbits. I've included information on their history, habitat, cages, enclosure, diet, facts, set up, food, names, pictures, information, lifespan, breeding, care sheet, feeding and cost. After reading this book you will be a lot more confident in looking after your Holland Lop Rabbit!

I have written this book using American spelling as that is what I'm used to. I have given measurements in both feet and inches/pounds and ounces and also in metric. I have also given costs in US$ and GBP. Both the measurements and costs are approximate guides. I have done my best to ensure the accuracy of the information in this book which was correct at the time of printing.

I trust that after reading this book you will feel more confident about owning and looking after a Holland Lop Rabbit and that you have a wonderful time enjoying the pleasure they bring in the years to come!

All good wishes, Ann L. Fletcher

Acknowledgements

I would like to thank my husband, John, who gave me my first Holland Lop, for his patience, love and understanding for my passion and love for these beautiful creatures. Who would have thought that a little rabbit could capture my heart and change my life but it certainly did.

Additional thanks to my children Mark and Stacey for their support in helping me to write this book. I'm delighted to share with them my love of rabbits that my late father instilled in me.

Table of Contents

Chapter One: Introduction

Holland Lop Rabbits are a wonderful breed of domestic rabbit. They are known for their long, pendulous ears and their friendly personalities. If you are looking for a new family pet this breed may be just what you are looking for. Not only are these animals wonderfully playful and entertaining, but they also tend to bond closely with their human caregivers.

The Holland Lop breed originated in the Netherlands and it has been recognized as a breed since 1964. These rabbits have a long history of careful breeding in Europe which has resulted in the beautiful and gentle breed they are today. Holland Lops are just as popular as house pets as they are for competition shows – breeders all across the United States and England compete to produce lops that fit the breed standard to a tee.

In reading this book you will learn everything you ever need to know about Holland Lop Rabbits including facts about the breed, the breed's history and information regarding the care of these wonderful creatures. If you are a new rabbit owner, you will also find helpful tips for finding a Holland Lop breeder, picking out a healthy rabbit and setting up your rabbit's cage for the first time. After reading this book you will be equipped with an in-depth knowledge of how to properly care for your Holland Lop Rabbits.

Useful Terms to Know:

- **Agouti**: patterned color; base color of dark grey, alternating bands of dark orange and tan

- **Buck**: a male rabbit

- **Cross Breeding**: breeding two different breeds together

- **Crown**: refers to a prominent ridge and crest along the top of the head extending to the base of the ears

- **Dam**: the mother of a rabbit

- **Doe**: a female rabbit

- **Hock**: the joint of the rabbit's foot

- **Inbreeding**: breeding two closely related rabbits to each other (i.e. brother to sister)

- **Junior**: young rabbit between 14 weeks and 5 months

- **Kindling**: process of giving birth to a litter of kits

- **Kit**: a baby rabbit

- **Litter**: two or more baby rabbits resulting from a single pregnancy/kindling

- **Lopped**: pendulous ears (opposite of erect ears)

- **Stud Buck**: a male rabbit suitable for breeding

- **Sire**: the father of a rabbit

- **Weaning**: the process through which kits begin to eat more solid food and rely less on nursing

1) What Are Holland Lop Rabbits?

The Holland Lop is a breed of domestic rabbit that originated in the Netherlands. Though the breed was recognized in its home country by the Netherlands' Governing Rabbit council in 1964, it wasn't until 1979 that it was recognized by the American Rabbit Breeders Association.

These rabbits are popular as family pets and they are also frequently bred for show. This breed is known for its sweet temperament and its long, drooping ears. Holland Lop

Rabbits remain fairly small and they have a stocky, rounded build. The fur of this breed is thick and soft and it comes in a variety of attractive colors.

What makes these rabbits so unique as pets is their friendly, almost dog-like personalities. Holland Lops can become very affectionate with their families – they can even be taught to play games. If allowed to roam freely in the house, a Holland Lop Rabbit is likely to follow you around, seeking your attention. If you are looking for a family-friendly pet, the Holland Lop Rabbit may be the perfect choice for you.

2) Facts about Holland Lop Rabbits

Holland Lop Rabbits are classified as a small breed. In the U.K., they are known as the Miniature Lop. This breed tends to achieve a maximum weight of around 4 lbs. (1.8 kg), though the breed standard indicates a maximum of 3.5 lbs. (1.5 kg). Though they may be small, the Holland Lop's thick coat gives is the appearance of being somewhat larger than it really is. These rabbits have densely furred coats that come in all colors and patterns.

The body of this breed is fairly compact and stocky in appearance. Holland Lops have short bodies with a well-muscled neck and a rounded rump. The front legs are short and straight while the hind legs are short and very strong. Both the legs and pads of the feet are well furred and the overall coat length is medium. The average lifespan of this breed is 7 to 9 years.

Summary of Holland Lop Rabbit Facts

Classification: small breed
Alternative Names: miniature lop (UK)
Weight: maximum 3.5 lbs. (1.5 kg)
Body Shape: rounded and short
Body Structure: stocky and compact
Coat Length: medium-length
Coat Color: any color or pattern
Lifespan: average 7 to 9 years

3) History of Holland Lop Rabbits as Pets

The development of the Holland Lop breed is credited to Adrian de Cock of Tilburg, Holland. It was his vision during the 1940s to create a miniaturized version of the French Lop. At the time, giant breeds like the French Lop were extremely popular throughout Europe but smaller breeds were uncommon.

Adrian de Cock began his breeding experiments in 1949 by crossing a French Lop buck with a Netherland Dwarf doe. Unfortunately, the resulting litter did not survive – the kits were abnormally large and the doe eventually died. It took another two years for Adrian to make another attempt at creating his miniature breed. In 1951, he bred a Netherland Dwarf buck to a French Lop doe. This breeding attempt was successful, resulting in 6 kits, all of which survived.

Netherland Dwarf Rabbit

All six kits from this first litter were kept and used to start the next generation. In 1952, Adrian bred a young doe to a Sooty Fawn buck. The litter produced only contained 3 kits but, unlike the first litter, all of the kits developed lopped ears. Adrian was extremely pleased with this litter and used them to continue the development of his breed.

By 1955, Adrian had achieved a number of successful breedings and a variety of colors. It wasn't until 1964, however, that the breed gained the interest of other breeders and was accepted by the Dutch authorities for standardization. A few years later, in 1970, breeders worked to decrease the maximum weight to the 1.5 kg it is today.

The Holland Lop breed was first brought to England in 1970 by George Scott of Yorkshire. In the following years, a number of Holland Lops were imported into the country and used for breeding. Several years later, in 1976, Aleck Brooks introduced the first Holland Lops into the United States. The breed was recognized by the American Rabbit Breeders Association in 1976. Since then, the breed has grown in popularity throughout the UK and US.

a) History of the British Rabbit Council

The breeding and showing of rabbits began over two hundred years ago. Throughout the nineteenth century, fanciers gathered to form local clubs for showing and improving individual breeds. The number of rabbit breeds recognized increased throughout the 1800s and early 1900s but by 1918, the most popular breed by far was the Beveren. In May of 1918 breeders of Beveren rabbits gathered to form a national club called The Beveren Club.

The Beveren Club served to raise the profile of rabbit breeding, adopting and standardizing new breeds. Eventually, the name of the club changed to the British Fur Rabbit Society and then to the British Rabbit Society. By 1928, over a dozen different breeds were recognized and interest in rabbit breeding began to grow. As a result, a new club was formed called the National Rabbit Council of Great Britain. The club grew quickly but conflicts arose between the two clubs which led to them eventually merging in 1934 to form the British Rabbit Council.

b) History of the American Rabbit Breeders' Association

The American Rabbit Breeders' Association (ARBA) was founded in 1910 and has its headquarters in Bloomington, Illinois. The purpose of this association is to promote rabbit fancy and to facilitate commercial rabbit production. The ARBA is responsible for setting breed standards and sanctioning rabbit shows throughout North America. In addition to sponsoring local clubs and fairs, the ARBA holds a national convention show annually, drawing rabbit fanciers from around the globe.

Not only does the ARBA set breed standards and organize shows, it also serves to provide rabbit raising education. Every five years the ARBA publishes a detailed guide for rabbit fanciers called *Standard of Perfection*. The ARBA also publishes educational materials like guidebooks and posters including photographs of all the recognized rabbit breeds. Additionally, the ARBA has a library of over 10,000 books and writings on domestic rabbits – the largest single repository of its kind.

4) *Types of Holland Lop Rabbits*

Baby Rabbits

Holland Lop Rabbits are born blind, deaf and hairless. At birth, newborn rabbits usually weigh no more than 1 or 1.5 oz. (45 to 68g) and because they have no hair, baby rabbits are extremely susceptible to cold. After a day or two they will begin to develop fuzz and by 1 ½ weeks of age their eyes and auditory canals will open. When they are born, Holland Lop kits typically have upright ears – their ears may not lop until they are 4 to 6 weeks old.

Holland Lop Rabbits sometimes give birth to deformed kits called "peanuts". These babies are the result of 2 dwarf genes and they generally die a few hours after birth. It is not difficult to identify a peanut because it will be visibly deformed and very different in appearance from regular kits. Peanuts oven have misshapen heads and unusually tiny ears. The limbs are also typically small and deformed.

Juvenile Rabbits

After Holland Rabbit kits open their eyes, they will also begin to move around the cage. At 3 weeks of age, most rabbit kits begin to sample solid food and they may also learn to use the water bottle. It is best to keep the kits with their mother until they are at least 4 weeks old – weaning is often done around 5 weeks of age. At this point, the mother should be removed from the cage but the babies can be kept together for a few more weeks.

Adult Rabbits

In adulthood, Holland Rabbits typically weigh a maximum of 4 lbs. (1.8 kg). Because they are small, this breed of rabbits matures more quickly than larger breeds. Holland Lops tend to reach sexual maturity between 3 and 5 months of age. Females of the breed tend to mature more quickly than males. To prevent unwanted breeding, it is best to separate the sexes around 2 months of age.

Male Rabbits

Male Holland Lops are called bucks. Because they tend to mature more slowly than females, Holland Lop bucks may not reach sexual maturity until they are 4 months of age or older. Even if they are capable of breeding this early, however, it is best to wait until the buck is 6 months old before breeding him.

If you attempt to breed a buck too early, it may not be successful and this could affect its future breeding potential. Young bucks should not be bred more than once a day and a maximum of 2 or 3 times per week. Once the buck reaches 1 year of age, however, it can be used several times in one day or once a day for several days in a row. Following repeated breedings, the male should be given a 5 to 7 day rest period.

Female Rabbits

Female Holland Lop Rabbits are called does. A Holland Lop doe typically reaches sexual maturity around 3 months of age, though some can become sexually mature sooner. This is why it is important to separate the sexes once they reach 2 months of age. It is best to wait until a doe is 6 months old before breeding her.

Once they become sexually mature, Holland Lop does are capable of producing a litter every 30 days or so – they can even be pregnant with two litters at once. A young doe will typically give birth to 1 to 3 kits in her first litter and generally between 2 and 4 in subsequent litters. As previously mentioned it is not uncommon for new mothers to give birth to stillborn kits or deformed kits called "peanuts."

5) Holland Lop Colors

Holland Lop Rabbits come in a variety of different colors and patterns. Show rabbits are classified by one of eight different patterns: agouti, broken, pointed white, self, shaded, ticked, tan and wide band. A variety of colors may be exhibited in each classification.

Agouti

An agouti pattern is one in which the top and side of the rabbit's body are banded and ticked with color. Ticked simply means that the tips of the hairs are a different color. There are several color variations for the agouti pattern including: chestnut, chocolate, chinchilla, chocolate chinchilla, lilac, opal and squirrel.

Broken

A broken pattern is simply any color combined with white – the body color should be broken evenly and there should be color on the nose, around each eye and on the ears. Ideally, broken lops should have between 10% and 70% color. Some of the color variations seen in broken lops include: black tri-color, blue tri-color, chocolate tri-color, lilac tri-color, Japanese harlequin and magpie harlequin.

Pointed White

Pointed white rabbits are also called Himalayans. These rabbits should have an overall body color of white with color points that may be black, blue, chocolate or lilac. Color points should be evident on the nose, ears and tail.

Self

The word "self" is used in regard to rabbits that exhibit a single color all over the body including its ears, head, feet and tail. Self-colored rabbits can be seen in black, white, chocolate, blue and lilac.

Shaded

Shaded Holland Lops exhibit darker coloring on the legs, feet, ears, tail and head with the color fading to a lighter shade on the body. Some of the color patterns seen in this category include: black tortoise, blue tortoise, chocolate tortoise, lilac tortoise, sable point, Siamese sable, seal and smoke pearl.

Ticked

Holland Lop Rabbits are said to be "ticked" when the tips of the hairs are a different color. These rabbits can be tipped with either gold or silver and the body color may be black, blue, chocolate or lilac.

Tan

The rabbits in this category exhibit a pattern called "otter". There are black otters, blue otters, chocolate otters and lilac otters. Rabbits in this group carry a tan gene instead of a self gene – the tan gene is dominant so it will show up if it is present in the rabbit's genetics.

Wide Band

Holland Lop Rabbits in the wide band category look very similar to those with the agouti pattern. Instead of the secondary color showing around the eyes, tail and ears, it shows in a layer – the rabbit will exhibit one color on top and a second on the bottom half of the body. Some of the colors seen in this category include: cream, fawn, orange, red and frosty.

Chapter Three: What to Know Before You Buy

1) Do You Need a License?

If you have done any research on keeping exotic pets, you may be aware that certain species require a permit or a license to keep. Domestic rabbits, however, are generally not considered to be exotic pets. This being the case, a license is generally not required to legally keep a Holland Lop Rabbit – certain regions do have legislation regarding the keeping and breeding of these pets so be sure to check with your local council. Even if your area does not require a license for keeping a rabbit, you may be subject to licensing requirements if you plan to breed or sell rabbits.

a) Licensing in the U.S.

There is no federal law in the United States requiring private rabbit owners to obtain a license for keeping Holland Lop Rabbits. There are, however, certain state laws regarding the keeping and breeding of domestic rabbits. The state of Minnesota, for example, requires rabbit owners to pay a $15 annual fee to license their pet rabbit – a higher fee may be charged if the rabbit is not spayed or neutered.

Generally, retail pet store owners and private collectors are not required to obtain a permit for keeping Holland Lop Rabbits. If you plan to breed your rabbits for wholesale or exhibition, however, you may need to obtain a license. To determine the requirements for your particular area, check with your local council. It is better to be safe than sorry – especially if failing to license your rabbit could cost you hefty fines.

b) Licensing in the U.K.

The U.K. does not have any legislation requiring rabbit owners or breeders to obtain a license. There are, however, laws in place in regard to importing or exporting animals.

Rabies has long been eradicated from the U.K. and strict import and export laws are now in place to prevent the disease from being re-introduced. If you plan to bring a rabbit with you to the U.K., or if you plan to export one, you will need to obtain an animal movement license (AML).

c) Licensing Elsewhere

Licensing requirements for Holland Lop Rabbits vary from one country or region to another. One of the only cases in which the ownership of pet rabbits is expressly prohibited is in Queensland, Australia. Rabbits are not a native species in Queensland – they are actually considered a Class 2 pest by the Land Protection Act of 2002.

Because they are not a native species, rabbits can threaten the survival of certain native species and also cause damage to the environment. It is not possible to obtain a permit to keep pet rabbits in Queensland for private purposes. The only time in which a permit may be issued is if the rabbit is being used for research or certain types of entertainment such as when used by magicians. The maximum penalty for keeping a rabbit without a license is Australian $40,000.

2) How Many Should You Buy?

If you perform a simple internet search on the subject of buying one or two rabbits, you are likely to receive mixed messages. While many rabbit owners advocate for keeping rabbits in pairs or colonies, an equally large number suggest that keeping a single rabbit is the better option. Before you go out and buy multiple rabbits, take the time to learn the positives and negatives of keeping a single rabbit versus a pair or colony.

You may have read that rabbits are social animals. This is true and it is based on the fact that rabbits live in colonies in the wild. It is important to note, however, that wild rabbits also follow a strict hierarchy and infringement of one rabbit into another's territory can cause problems. Keeping two rabbits in a single cage has the potential to cause problems as well. If one rabbit is more dominant than the other, the subservient rabbit might be bullied or chased around the cage. Eventually, the stress of this living situation could have negative repercussions on your rabbit's health.

Rabbit owners who advocate for keeping a single rabbit also suggest that Holland Lop Rabbits are more likely to bond with their human caretakers if they are kept on their own. While rabbits may bond with other rabbits, they are just as likely to bond with a human or another species. As long as you fulfill your rabbit's basic needs and give him plenty of attention, he will be perfectly happy on his own. Studies of wild rabbits have shown that they are perfectly capable of living in isolation from other rabbits – they may even enjoy a longer lifespan because they are not affected by the stress of dealing with bullies.

If you do plan to keep two rabbits together, it is best to buy them and introduce them when they are the same age. Do not assume that two rabbits will get along just because they were born in the same litter – it all depends on individual personality and temperament. When you first introduce your rabbits, supervise them to make sure they get along. If one of the rabbits begins chasing the other you should separate them – it is not likely that they will eventually "work out their differences." It is more likely that one rabbit will end up seriously injuring the other.

3) Can Holland Lop Rabbits Be Kept with Other Pets?

Holland Lop Rabbits are capable of being kept with a variety of different pets. These rabbits are not aggressive or combative by nature, so it really depends on the other pet. These rabbits can even get along with dogs, as long as the dog has a gentle temperament. If you do plan to keep your rabbit with other pets, just be sure to supervise their time together to prevent any accidents.

My best advice is not to take any chances but ultimately you must make a judgment call as you are best placed to know the character of your pets.

Tips for Keeping Rabbits with Other Pets

- Always supervise your Holland Lop's time with other pets to prevent accidents

- Make sure your rabbit has a safe place to retreat to if he wants to

- Holland Lops can bond with a variety of pets including cats, dogs and guinea pigs

- Do not keep Holland Lops with ferrets – ferrets are predatory animals and may injure your rabbit

- Holland Lops are compatible with pets that are kept in tanks (e.g. fish and frogs) as long as you prevent them from chewing on electrical cords

- Rabbits may not get along with birds – due to their sensitive ears, noisy birds may irritate rabbits

  **Note: If you plan to let your rabbit roam freely outside the cage, be sure to keep him from getting into other pets' foods.

4) Ease and Cost of Care

Holland Lop Rabbits are an excellent choice for a family pet
because they are gentle, friendly and love to have the
attention of their human companions. Before you go out
and buy a rabbit, however, you should be sure that you can
handle the initial and ongoing monthly costs.

The initial costs of a Holland Lop Rabbit include the
purchase price of the rabbit itself plus the cost of
spay/neuter surgery, microchipping and initial vaccinations
as well as the cost of the cage and accessories. Once you
cover these overheads you must also think about monthly
expenses such as food, bedding and veterinary care. Think
about all of these expenses before you decide to buy a
Holland Lop Rabbit.

a) Initial Costs

Initial costs for keeping a Holland Lop Rabbit are those
required to buy your rabbit and to prepare its cage. In
addition to the cage and the rabbit itself you will need to
pay for de-sexing and microchipping the rabbit as well as
any initial vaccinations the rabbit needs. Add to these the
cost of preparing the rabbit's cage and stocking up on

accessories and you will find the initial costs of keeping a Holland Lop Rabbit.

Purchase Price: The price of a Holland Lop Rabbit will vary depending where you buy it. You may be able to find these rabbits at your local pet store for around $20 to $25 (£13 - £16.25). These rabbits are not guaranteed to be pedigreed, however. Pedigreed Holland Lop Rabbits bred for show tend to be more expensive than other rabbits – they can cost as much as $40 to $60 (£26 to £39).

Spay/Neuter: It is always a good idea to have your Holland Lop Rabbits spayed or neutered. If you do not plan to breed your rabbits, it is particularly important that you do this. The cost of spay/neuter surgery is generally around $100 (£65) but you may be able to find a lower price if there is a veterinary clinic in your area.

Microchipping: A microchip is a tiny electronic device that is inserted under your rabbit's skin. This device is used to store your contact information so if the rabbit is lost, you can be contacted. It is not a requirement that you have your rabbit microchipped, but it is certainly a good idea. The cost of this procedure is generally about $30 (£19.50).

Vaccinations: One of the first things you need to do when you get a new rabbit is to have it examined by a veterinarian and caught up on its vaccinations. Costs for veterinary care may vary depending where you live but the average cost for initial vaccinations is around $50-$65 (£32.50 to £42.25).

Cage: Holland Lop Rabbits are a very small breed, weighing a maximum of 4 lbs. (1.8kg) at maturity. This being the case, they do not require a very large cage. It is important, however, that you provide your rabbits with plenty of space to hop around and stretch out. You may also choose to let your rabbit roam free throughout the house. Even if you do that, you should have a cage or hutch where your rabbit can sleep at night. The cost for a rabbit's cage will vary depending on size and materials but you should be ready to spend around $200 to $300 (£130 - £195).

Accessories: To prepare your rabbit's cage you will need to stock up on a few accessories. These accessories might include a water bottle, food bowl, bedding and chew toys for your rabbit. Another accessory that would be good to have around is a travel carrier – this will be useful when you need to take your rabbit to the vet. The cost of initial accessories may be around $100 (£65).

Additional Costs: In addition to purchasing your rabbit as well as his cage and accessories, there are a few additional costs you should be prepared for. Some of these costs might include a litter pan, grooming supplies and cleaning equipment. For the most part, these tools and supplies should last you for several years and the total cost may average around $100 (£65).

Summary of Initial Costs:

Cost Type	One Rabbit	Two Rabbits
Purchase Price	$20 - $60 (£13 - £39)	$40 to $120 (£26 - £78)
Spay/Neuter	$100 (£65)	$200 (£130)
Microchipping	$30 (£19.50)	$60 (£39)
Vaccinations	$50 (£32.50)	$100 (£65)
Cage or Pen	$200 to $300 (£130 - £195)	$200 to $300 (£130 - £195)
Cage Accessories	$100 (£65)	$100 (£65)
Other Tools/Equipment	$100 (£65)	$100 (£65)
Total:	$600 - $740 (£390 - £481)	$800 - $980 (£520 - £637)

b) Monthly Costs

In addition to these initial costs, you should also be ready to pay for several other expenses on a monthly basis. In order to properly care for your Holland Lop Rabbit you will need to buy fresh food and bedding every month – you may also need to provide routine veterinary care. Additionally, you should be prepared to pay for additional costs such as replacing accessories or making repairs to the cage. Below you will find an explanation of the monthly overheads you can come to expect as a Holland Lop Rabbit owner.

Food: Your monthly costs for rabbit food will vary depending how many rabbits you keep and what type of food you buy. Some of the types of food you will need to buy for your rabbits include greens, hay, commercial rabbit pellets and fresh vegetables. The cost to feed a single Holland Lop Rabbit for one month averages about $30 (£19.50).

Bedding: If you plan to keep your rabbit in its cage or hutch, your bedding costs may be higher than if you let your rabbit roam free throughout the house. Your monthly cost for bedding will also depend on the type of bedding you buy. In general, you should plan to spend up to $50

(£32.50) per month on this. You can reduce your bedding costs by using recycled newspapers, but do not use colored magazines because the ink may contain toxins that are harmful to your rabbit.

Veterinary Care: If you look after your Holland Lop properly, you should not have to worry about veterinary care on a monthly basis. You should, however, take your rabbit to the vet for a check-up once a year. The total yearly cost for this is generally around $50 (£32.50) which averages to less than $5 (£3.25) per month.

Additional Costs: You should allow for some small monthly costs $25 (£16.25) per year which averages to less than $3 (£1.95) per month to replace chew toys, treats and making repairs to the cage etc.

Summary of Monthly Costs:

Cost Type	One Rabbit	Two Rabbits
Food	$30 (£19.50)	$60 (£39.00)
Bedding	$50 (£32.50)	$50 (£32.50)
Veterinary Care	$5 (£3.25)	$10 (£6.50)
Additional Costs	$3 (£1.95)	$6 (£3.90)
Total:	$88 (£57.20)	$126 (£81.90)

5) Pros and Cons of Holland Lop Rabbits

As is true of any pet, keeping a Holland Lop Rabbit has its pros and cons. Before you go out and buy a rabbit, take the time to learn the ups and downs of this breed to be sure that it is the right choice for you.

Pros for Holland Lop Rabbits

- Holland Lops are quiet pets and naturally friendly
- Rabbits can bond with human companions
- Can be compatible with other pets if properly supervised
- Holland Lops are very playful and fun to have around the house
- Rabbits can be litter trained, makes clean-up easier

Cons for Holland Lop Rabbits

- Rabbits are a long-term commitment – they are just as much work to care for as a dog or cat
- Dietary needs of Holland Lops are very specific

- Rabbits can do damage in the house with chewing if not supervised properly
- Do not do well in isolation – require plenty of care and interaction with owners
- Require plenty of chew toys to keep teeth filed down
- Holland Lops often prefer not to be held – may not be a good choice for eager children

Chapter Four: Purchasing Holland Lop Rabbits

1) Where to Buy Holland Lop Rabbits

If you have decided that a Holland Lop Rabbit is definitely the right pet for you, you can then begin looking for a rabbit to purchase. Where you purchase your rabbit will have a significant impact on the health and breeding of your rabbit. If you do not purchase from a reputable source, you cannot be sure that the rabbit you are bringing home is healthy. Take precautions in locating a breeder and always make sure the breeder is experienced in breeding and caring for Holland Lop Rabbits.

a) Buying in the U.S.

In the United States, you may be able to find Holland Lop Rabbits at your local pet store. Keep in mind, however, that rabbits sold at pet stores may not be bred from high-quality stock and they may be more likely to be exposed to disease. Even if you do not buy from the pet store, you may still be able to get information about local breeders in your area. You might also try asking your veterinarian for a referral.

Another option is to perform an online search for Holland Lop Rabbit breeders in your area. You can often find listings of breeders on national websites such as the American Rabbit Breeders Association or the Holland Lop Specialty Club. If all else fails, look for a rabbit rescue center in your area. You may not find a center that has baby rabbits available, but adult rabbits are likely to already be litter trained and are more likely to be caught up on vaccinations. It's always gives you a good feeling to help rehouse an abandoned pet.

The websites on the following pages will provide you with additional information and contacts in your local area: -

U.S. Breeder Websites:

"ARBA Breeder Listing." American Rabbit Breeders Association, Inc. www.arba.net/breeders.htm

"Holland Lop Rabbit Breeders." RabbitBreeders.us. http://rabbitbreeders.us/holland-lop-rabbit-breeders

"Locate a Breeder." Holland Lop Rabbit Specialty Club. www.hlrsc.com/

b) Buying in the U.K.

You might be able to find Holland Lop Rabbits at your local pet store in the U.K. As is true in the U.S., you should be aware that rabbits sold at pet stores may not be bred from high-quality stock. If you don't want to buy from a pet store, ask your veterinarian or fellow rabbit owners for a referral to a breeder. Another option is to check the breeder listings on the British Rabbit Council or National Miniature Lop Rabbit Club websites. Your local RSPCA may have some rescue rabbits available.

U.K. Breeder Websites:

"Members and Breeders Websites." The Northern Lop Club. www.thenorthernlopclub.co.uk/5.html

"Breeder Links." National Miniature Lop Rabbit Club. www.nmlrc.co.uk/links.htm

"Breeders Directory." The British Rabbit Council. www.thebrc.org/breeders-list.htm

**Note: Purchasing animals online is dangerous and can be considered cruel because it is difficult to regulate the treatment of animals during shipping – they may be exposed to extreme temperatures and/or rough handling. Please avoid buying Holland Lop Rabbits online. In fact, if this is your only option, then please reconsider having a pet at all. It just isn't worth it!

2) How to Select a Healthy Holland Lop Rabbit

Unfortunately, many novice rabbit owners make the mistake of bringing home a Holland Lop Rabbit that isn't completely healthy. If your new rabbit is already suffering from disease, the stress of the move and acclimating to a new environment could be extremely dangerous. To avoid the heartache of losing your new rabbit, take the time to make sure the rabbit you bring home is healthy.

Follow these tips to make sure you bring home a healthy Holland Lop Rabbit:

Do your research.

Shop around for a reputable breeder and take the time to interview each breeder. Ask questions to ascertain the breeder's knowledge of and experience with the Holland Lop Breed. If the breeder can't answer your questions or appears to be avoiding them, move on to another breeder.

Ask for a tour.

Once you select a breeder, pay a visit to the facilities. Ask to see the places where the rabbits are kept and ask to see the parents of the litter from which you are buying. If the facilities are dirty or the parents appear to be in poor health, do not purchase a rabbit from that breeder.

Observe the kits.

If the facilities and parents appear to be in good order, ask to see the litter of rabbits. Observe their appearance and activity to see if they look healthy. Healthy Holland Lops should be active and curious, not hiding in a corner or acting lethargic.

Examine the rabbits individually.

If the litter appears to be in good condition, pick out a few of the rabbits that you like. Handle the rabbits briefly to see how they react to human interaction and check them for obvious signs of disease and injury. Check the rabbit's ears and nose for discharge and make sure that the eyes are bright and clear. The rabbit's teeth should be straight and its coat healthy.

If, after touring the facilities and ensuring that the rabbits themselves are healthy, you can begin negotiations with the breeder. Make sure you get the rabbit's medical history and breeding information for your own records. Ask if the rabbit comes with a health guarantee and make sure you get all the paperwork necessary to register your rabbit, should you choose to do so.

Chapter Five: Caring for Holland Ka.

1) Habitat Requirements

The most important aspect of choosing a habitat for your Holland Lop is space – if your rabbit doesn't have adequate space to hop, run and stretch out, then it could succumb to both physical and behavioral disorders. Ideally, your rabbit should only spend part of the day in his cage – the rest of his time should be spent roaming the house or in an open exercise pen. Your rabbit's cage can be kept indoors or outside but, as you will learn in this chapter, keeping rabbits outdoors does have its risks.

a) Choosing a Cage

There are a number of factors to consider when choosing a cage for your Holland Lop. Though these rabbits do remain fairly small, they still need to have plenty of space in their cage. A cage for Holland Lops should be long enough that your rabbit can make three or four hops from one end to the other. The cage should be wide enough that your rabbit can stretch out across the width and tall enough that it can stand on its hind legs.

An open exercise pen or rabbit run can be as large as you like but the walls should be at least 3 feet (1 meter) high so your bunny doesn't escape. You may also want to bury the wire at least a few inches underground to prevent your rabbit from digging under it. I strongly recommend that you might also want to make sure the top of the pen is covered so predators cannot get in to attack your rabbit. Another thing you need to think about when keeping your rabbit in an exercise pen outdoors is that you should cover about half of the pen with a towel or another solid object to provide your rabbit with shade.

In addition to the size, you also need to think about the materials from which your rabbit cage is built. Metal cages made from wire mesh with a solid bottom are best. Cages that have wire mesh bottoms may make clean-up easier by allowing feces to fall through the holes, but it can also hurt your rabbit's feet. It is far better to clean out your rabbit's cage often enough that the bedding remains fresh.

In terms of bedding, the best kinds to use are non-toxic pelleted litter, fresh hay or newspaper. The dyes and inks used in the vast majority of newspapers today are made from soy based inks. Pine and cedar shavings can cause irritation and both clay and clumping cat litters can be harmful to rabbits. You should also avoid using colored magazine pages as bedding because the ink on the pages may be toxic – it could be dangerous for your rabbit if he eats it.

b) Indoors vs. Outdoors

Whether you keep your Holland Lop Rabbit indoors or outdoors is your choice, but you would be wise to learn the pros and cons of both options before you make a decision. I've listed some of these for you to consider on the next few pages:

Pros for Indoor Rabbits

- Not exposed to inclement weather or predators
- Less likely to come into contact with parasites
- More likely to receive adequate attention and interaction with human caregivers
- More likely to form a bond with owners
- Longer lifespan, less susceptible to disease

Cons for Indoor Rabbits

- Cage takes up space in the home
- Free-roaming rabbits may be underfoot – could potentially be injured
- Noise and odor is more noticeable if cage isn't cleaned often enough
- Free-roaming rabbits may chew on electrical cords, furniture, etc.
- Litter training is a definite requirement

Pros for Outdoor Rabbits

- Easier to accommodate large cages and multiple Holland Lop Rabbits
- Odor and noise are not an issue
- In rabbit runs, rabbits can eat grass and other plants
- More space for rabbits to stretch out and exercise
- Clean-up can be much easier, may not even need to litter train rabbits

Cons for Outdoor Rabbits

- Rabbits may not receive as much human interaction
- May be less likely to form a bond with human caretakers and pets
- More likely to be exposed to parasites and other dangerous diseases
- At risk of attack by predators
- May be exposed to inclement weather and extreme temperatures
- Cannot monitor what they are eating as easily

c) Single vs. Multi-Level

In addition to deciding whether you want to keep your rabbit indoors or outdoors, you also need to think about what kind of cage you want to provide it with. Indoor cages come in two main varieties: single-level and multi-level. Multi-level cages are also referred to as rabbit condos and they provide vertical space as well as horizontal space.

The main difference between these two options is the amount of space they provide. With a single-level cage, the only way to provide more space is to increase the length and width dimensions of the cage – the larger the cage, the more space it takes up in your house. A multi-level cage, on the other hand, provides extra space by adding different levels. You can arrange your multi-level cage so that the litter pan is on the bottom with the food and resting while playing areas are on the upper floors.

No matter which option you choose, you should also think about how you are going to provide your rabbit with free space. Ideally, your rabbit should only spend a few hours a day (most likely at night) in his cage – the rest of the time he should be allowed to roam freely or given time in an open enclosure or rabbit run. To build your own rabbit run, all you need are a few interlocking mesh panels. You can also build a wooden frame and cover the sides with wire mesh. If you use your rabbit run outdoors, be sure to provide your rabbits with an area of shade.

d) Cage Accessories

Rabbits do not require a great many accessories for their cages. The basic necessities include:

- Water Bottle
- Food Bowl(s)
- Hay Compartment
- Litter Pan
- Chew Toys
- Nest Box or Shelter
- Other Toys

Toys for Holland Lop Rabbits do not need to be extravagant – they do not even need to be store-bought! You can make your own rabbit toys at home out of cardboard tubes, boxes, plastic balls, wooden blocks and whatever else you have on hand! Please ensure that any materials used are non-toxic and BPA free.

2) Feeding Holland Lop Rabbits

The health and wellness of your Holland Lop Rabbit is largely dependent on what you feed it. Offering your rabbit a varied diet of rabbit pellets, Timothy hay and vegetables is the key to keeping your rabbit in good condition. If you feed your rabbit low-quality feed or do not supplement his diet with fresh vegetables or hay, he may fail to thrive and might even lose some of his condition. In this chapter you will learn what you need to know about feeding your Holland Lops.

a) Nutritional Needs

Holland Lop Rabbits require a diet that is low in protein and high in fiber. The majority of your rabbit's diet should be made up of high-quality feed, also called pellets. Do not just grab a bag of rabbit pellets off the shelf – not all rabbit pellets are created equal. It is important that you take the time to review the ingredients list on the package to determine whether it is a good quality food to offer your rabbit. Ideally, rabbit pellets should contain no more than 16% protein and at least 20% to 25% fiber.

The main ingredient in your rabbit's pellets should be alfalfa – if it is first on the ingredients list that means it is the main ingredient by concentration. If you purchase a low-quality feed, you may be purchasing a produce that consists mainly of feed dust or one that contains artificial "binders". You should also be sure that the feed is free from corn and growth hormones.

When reading the food labels on your rabbit's pellets, you should look to determine what type of grain is used. The two most commonly used grains in rabbit pellets are oats and barley. Corn is not ideal, though very small amounts in the feed are unlikely to cause any negative effects. Many Holland Lops prefer oat formulas over barley formulas but your rabbit's preferences may be different. If you want to try out different types of feed, be sure to make the transition slowly so it doesn't upset your rabbit's stomach.

b) Supplemental Foods

In addition to pellets, you should also supply your rabbit with an unlimited quantity of Timothy hay. Timothy hay is high in fiber which will help prevent hairballs from forming in the rabbit's stomach as it grooms itself. If you like to give your rabbit treats, you can offer it small amounts of fresh fruits and vegetables. Holland Lops tend to enjoy lettuce, broccoli, carrots, cabbage, bananas and apples. Just be sure not to feed too much of these foods because it can upset your rabbit's sensitive stomach.

Tips for Feeding Holland Lops:

- Choose a certain time of day to feed your rabbits or divide their food into two daily meals (rabbits appreciate routine)

- Make any dietary changes slowly – drastic changes in feed can cause severe digestive problems

- Always use pellets within 60 days of manufacture (not purchase)

- Check your feed often for signs of mold or foul odor – these signs indicate that the feed has gone bad

- Trust your rabbits – if they suddenly stop eating the feed there may be something wrong with it and you should remove it immediately

- If they stop eating and it isn't the food, they may be ill, so watch them carefully and take them to the vet if you are concerned

- Always keep an unlimited supply of fresh water available for your rabbits – dehydration can cause severe health problems

- Avoid commercially produced rabbit treats because they are rarely healthy

c) How Much to Feed

The amount of food you give your rabbit on a daily basis depends on its age and weight. Rabbits that have been weaned should be given unlimited access to pellets until they reach 6 months of age. During this time you can also offer your baby rabbits Timothy or meadow hay . It is not a good idea, however, to give your baby rabbits too many vegetables because it can upset their stomachs. At the most, offer your baby and junior rabbits one piece of fruit or vegetable per day (teaspoon size) and introduce them one at a time.

Once your rabbit reaches 6 months of age you can begin feeding it a limited amount of rabbit feed. Holland Lop Rabbits should be fed 1 oz. of feed per pound of body weight (0.45 kg). Holland Lops weigh an average of 4 lbs. (1.8 kg) which means they need about 4 oz. (1.81kg) of feed, or about ½ cup, per day. You may choose whether you want to offer all of this food at once or if you want to divide it into two separate feedings. In addition to the pellets, you should also make sure your rabbits have an unlimited supply of Timothy or meadow hay and fresh water.

d) Good vs. Bad Foods

There are certain foods and plants which can be very harmful for your Holland Lop Rabbit. Before you feed your rabbit anything besides Timothy hay or pellets, check this list.

Plants Toxic for Rabbits:

Acorns	Lily of the Valley
Aloe	Marigold
Apple Seeds	Milkweed
Almonds	Mistletoe
Asparagus Fern	Nutmeg
Azalea	Oak
Carnations	Juniper
Clematis	Jack-in-the-Pulpit
Daffodil Bulbs	Laurel
Eucalyptus	Lupin
Fruit Pits	Parsnip
Fruit Seeds	Poppy
Geranium	Peony
Gladiola	Philodendron
Hemlock	Poinsettia
Hyacinth Bulbs	Rhubarb Leaves
Impatiens	Sweet Potato
Iris	Tansy

Ivy

Jasmine

Jessamine

Tomato Leaves

Tulip Bulbs

Violet

Yew

This list is not comprehensive; in order to determine whether a specific plant is toxic for rabbits, consult the House Rabbit Society website: http://rabbit.org/poisonous-plants/

Foods Good for Rabbits:

Apples

Beans

Blueberries

Carrots

Cherries

Dandelion Greens

Grapes

Kale

Mustard Greens

Mango

Melon

Orange

Pear

Papaya

Pineapple

Peach

Peas

Parsnip

Parsley

Raspberries

Strawberries

Tomatoes (fruit)

3) Litter Training a Rabbit

In many cases, rabbits will litter train themselves because
they are naturally clean animals. If you do need to litter
train your rabbit, however, it is not difficult to do. You will
need to start by isolating your rabbit in a small area without
carpeting (this will make it easier to clean up any mess).

Next, prepare a litter box that is large enough for your
rabbit to lie down in. Fill the litter box with about 1 inch of
non-toxic litter and cover it with a layer of hay. If you can,
take some of the soiled hay from your rabbit's cage and add
it to the litter box to encourage your rabbit to use it. Confine
your rabbit to the area with the litter box until he begins to
urinate exclusively in the litter box.

Another option is to place multiple litter boxes in your
rabbit's cage. Keep an eye on your rabbit and take note of
which areas he tends to choose to do his business. Keep the
litter boxes in those areas and remove the rest. Your rabbit
might have a few accidents outside the litter box now and
then but this is normal behavior.
Note: Certain types of litter are harmful to Holland Lop
Rabbits including clay litter, clumping litter, pine or cedar
shavings and corn cob litter.

Chapter Six: Health Issues

1) *Common Health Problems*

** Note: This section may be upsetting to any children who may read it. Sadly like all our pets, Holland Lop Rabbits are susceptible to developing certain health issues.

In order to keep your rabbit healthy you need to ensure its cage is kept clean and offer it a varied, high-quality diet. You should also familiarize yourself with some of the most common health problems so you will be better prepared to identify them and seek treatment before it is too late. The details in this section are not designed to take the place of a qualified veterinarian who will have up to date knowledge and information regarding current treatments for any ailments. While some health conditions can be treated at home please ensure that if there is any condition that is impacting your rabbit's health or mobility, you do not delay in taking it to your vet. Some of the common health issues are:

- Myxomatosis
- Viral Hemorrhagic Disease
- Pneumonia
- Otitis Media
- Listeriosis
- Dermatophytosis
- Mastitis
- Colibacillosis
- Enterotoxemia
- Rhinitis
- Papillomatosis
- Dental Problems
- Parasites
- Uterine Cancer
- Fleas/Mites

Myxomatosis

Myxomatosis is a viral disease that is caused by myxoma virus. This condition is typically fatal and it can be transmitted through direct contact or through biting insects. Some of the initial symptoms of the disease include conjunctivitis, eye discharge, listlessness, anorexia and fever. In severe cases, death may occur after only 48 hours.

Treatment for this condition is generally not effective and it can cause severe and lasting damage. There is however, a vaccine available against myxomatosis. This vaccine should be given after the rabbit reaches 6 weeks of age.

Causes: by myxoma virus; transmitted through direct contact or through biting insects
Symptoms: conjunctivitis, eye discharge, listlessness, anorexia and fever
Treatment: generally not effective; vaccine is available

Viral Hemorrhagic Disease

Also called rabbit hemorrhagic disease, viral hemorrhagic disease is transmitted through direct contact or contaminated food, water and bedding. Unfortunately, there is no effective treatment for this condition and many rabbits die from it without ever showing symptoms.

Some of the most common symptoms of viral hemorrhagic disease include difficulty breathing, paralysis, lethargy, bloody discharge from the nose, weight loss and convulsions. Once symptoms appear, the disease is typically fatal within 2 weeks.

Causes: rabbit calcivirus; transmitted through direct contact or contaminated food, water and bedding
Symptoms: difficulty breathing, paralysis, lethargy, bloody discharge from the nose, weight loss and convulsions
Treatment: no effective treatment

Pneumonia

Pneumonia is fairly common in domestic rabbits and it is most often a secondary infection. The most common cause of pneumonia in rabbits is *P multocida* bacteria, though other kinds may be involved. A precursor of pneumonia is often upper respiratory disease which may be a result of inadequate ventilation or sanitation.

Some of the common symptoms of pneumonia include listlessness, fever and anorexia. Once they show symptoms, most rabbits succumb to the infection within 1 week. Though antibiotic treatment is often used, it is not typically effective because it may not be administered until the disease is highly advanced.

Causes: *P multocida* bacteria
Symptoms: listlessness, fever and anorexia
Treatment: antibiotic treatment is often used but not typically effective

Otitis Media

Also called "wry neck" or "head tilt," otitis media is caused by an infection resulting from *P multocida* or *Encephalitozoon cunuculi*. These bacteria cause the accumulation of fluid or pus in the ear, causing the rabbit to tilt its head. Antibiotic therapy may be effective, though it may just worsen the condition. In most cases, rabbits infected with this condition are culled.

Causes: *P multocida* or *Encephalitozoon cunuculi* bacteria
Symptoms: accumulation of fluid or pus in the ear, causing the rabbit to tilt its head
Treatment: antibiotic therapy may be effective

Listeriosis

Listeriosis is a type of sporadic septicemia which often causes sudden death or abortion – this condition is most common in pregnant does. Some of the contributing factors for this disease include poor husbandry and stress. Some of the common symptoms include anorexia, depression and weight loss.

If not properly treated, the *Listeria monocytogenes* responsible for the disease can spread to the blood, liver and uterus. Treatment is not often attempted because diagnosis is not frequently made premortem.

Causes: *Listeria monocytogenes*
Symptoms: anorexia, depression and weight loss; often causes sudden death or abortion
Treatment: not often attempted because diagnosis is not frequently made premortem

Dermatophytosis

Also known as ringworm, dermatophytosisis caused by either *Trichophyton mentagrophytes* or *Microsporum canis*. These infections typically result from poor husbandry or inadequate nutrition. Ringworm can be transmitted through direct contact with an infected rabbit or sharing tools such as brushes.

The symptoms of ringworm include circular raised bumps on the body. The skin is these areas may be red and capped with a white, flaky material. Some of the most common treatments for ring worm include topical antifungal creams that contain miconazole or itraconazole. A 1% copper sulfate dip may also be effective.

Causes: *Trichophyton mentagrophytes* or *Microsporum canis*; typically results from poor husbandry or inadequate nutrition

Symptoms: circular raised bumps on the body; skin is red and capped with a white, flaky material

Treatment: include topical antifungal creams that contain miconazole or itraconazole; 1% copper sulfate dip

Mastitis

This condition is most commonly seen in rabbitries but it can affect single rabbits. Mastitis is a condition that affects pregnant does and it is caused by staphylococci bacteria. The bacteria infect the mammary glands, causing them to become hot, red and swollen. If the disease is allowed to progress, it may cause septicemia and become fatal.

Does affected by mastitis are unlikely to eat but they will crave water. The rabbit may also run a fever. Treatment for this condition may include antibiotic treatment. Penicillin, however, should be avoided because it can cause diarrhea. Kits should not be fostered because they will only end up spreading the disease.

Causes: staphylococci bacteria
Symptoms: hot, red and swollen mammary glands; loss of appetite; fever
Treatment: antibiotics

Colibacillosis

Colibacillosis is characterized by severe diarrhea and it is often caused by *Escherichia coli*. This disease can be seen in two forms depending on the rabbit's age. Newborn rabbits may exhibit a yellowish diarrhea – in newborns, this condition is often fatal and can affect the entire litter. In weaned rabbits, the intestines may fill with fluid and hemorrhages may surface.

In the case of weaned rabbits, the disease is typically fatal within 2 weeks. If the rabbit survives, it is likely to be stunted. Treatment is not often successful but, in mild cases, antibiotics may help. Rabbits that are severely affected with this disease should be culled to avoid the spread of the disease.

Causes: *Escherichia coli*
Symptoms: yellowish diarrhea in newborns; fluid-filled intestines and hemorrhages in weaned rabbits
Treatment: antibiotics; treatment is not often effective

Enterotoxemia

Enterotoxemia is a disease characterized by explosive diarrhea and it typically affects rabbits between the ages of 4 and 8 weeks. Symptoms of this condition include lethargy, loss of condition and greenish-brown fecal matter around the perianal area. In many cases, this condition is fatal within 48 hours.

The primary cause of this disease is *Clostridium spiroforme*. These organisms are common in rabbits in small numbers but they can become a problem when the rabbit's diet is too low in fiber. Treatment may not be effective due to the rapid progression of the disease but adding cholestryamine or copper sulfate to the diet can help prevent enterotoxemia. Reducing stress in young rabbits and increasing fiber intake can also help.

Causes: *Clostridium spiroforme*
Symptoms: lethargy, loss of condition and greenish-brown fecal matter around the perianal area
Treatment: may not be effective; adding cholestryamine or copper sulfate to the diet can help prevent

Rhinitis

Rhinitis is the medical term used to describe sniffling or chronic inflammation in the airway and lungs. This condition is often caused by *Pastuerella*, though *Staphylococcus* or *Streptococcus* may also be involved. The initial symptom of this disease is a thin stream of mucus flowing from the nose. As the disease progresses, the flow may encrust the fur on the paws and chest. Sneezing and coughing may also be exhibited. This condition generally resolves itself but even recovered rabbits can be carriers of the disease.

Causes: is often caused by *Pastuerella*, though *Staphylococcus* or *Streptococcus* may also be involved
Symptoms: sniffling or chronic inflammation in the airway and lungs; thin stream of mucus flowing from the nose
Treatment: generally resolves itself

Papillomatosis

Papillomatosis is fairly common in domestic rabbits and it is caused by the rabbit oral papillomavirus. This disease results in the formation of small grey nodules or warts on the underside of the tongue or floor of the mouth. Another type, caused by cottontail papillomavirus, may produce horned warts on the neck, shoulders, ears and abdomen. There is no treatment for these conditions but the lesions typically go away on their own in time.

Causes: rabbit oral papillomavirus
Symptoms: small grey nodules or warts on the underside of the tongue or floor of the mouth
Treatment: no treatment; the lesions typically go away on their own in time

Dental Problems

All rabbits, including Holland Lops, are prone to developing dental problems. The most common issues are overgrown molars and enamel spurs. Your rabbit's teeth may become overgrown or develop spurs if you don't provide enough fiber-rich foods. If your rabbit's teeth are not properly aligned they can develop a condition called malocclusion. There are three main causes of this, the most common being genetic predisposition, injury, or bacterial infection. If you provide your rabbit with adequate chew toys, you shouldn't have to worry about its teeth becoming overgrown. You should, however, make frequent checks to see if the teeth are properly aligned – if they aren't, your rabbit could develop molar spurs or abscesses in the mouth.

Fibrous foods are naturally abrasive which helps to keep your rabbit's teeth filed down. In most cases, dental problems require veterinary treatment.

Causes: diet too low in fiber
Symptoms: overgrown molars, enamel spurs
Treatment: veterinary exam and treatment

Parasites

One of the most common parasites found in Holland Lop Rabbits is Encephalitozoon cuniculi. This protozoan parasite can survive in the body for years without causing any harm. In some cases, however, the parasite can cause severe damage. This parasite typically causes nerve damage which results in head tilting, incontinence, paralysis and rupture of the lens of the eye.

Intestinal worms are also a common problem in rabbits. Both of these conditions can be treated with de-worming paste. This treatment can be used for infected rabbits and as a preventive against parasites. When used as a preventive, the paste is typically administered twice a year.

Causes: Encephalitozoon cuniculi, intestinal worms
Symptoms: head tilting, incontinence, paralysis and rupture of the lens of the eye
Treatment: de-worming paste

Uterine Cancer

A common cause of death in female rabbits, uterine cancer can easily be prevented. Spaying female rabbits between the ages of 5 months and 2 years is the best way to prevent this disease. In un-spayed female rabbits, uterine cancer can spread to several different organs before the disease is diagnosed. At that point, treatment is typically ineffective.

Causes: tumor growing in the uterus

Symptoms: other reproductive issues; endometriosis, bulging veins, vaginal discharge, bloody urine

Treatment: spaying female rabbits to prevent; once the cancer develops, treatment is generally ineffective

Fleas/Mites

Indoor rabbits are unlikely to contract fleas and ticks on their own. If your rabbit spends time outside or if you have other pets that spend time outside, however, your rabbit could be at risk. Mites are typically found in the ears and fur of rabbits and they most often present themselves after your rabbit's immune system has already been compromised.

Fur mites tend to stay at the base of the neck or near the rabbit's rear. If left untreated, mites and fleas can cause severe itching, bald spots and bleeding. The best treatment for fleas and mites is a prescription medication called Revolution, known in the UK as Stronghold. Another treatment option in the UK is Ivermectin drops. Be sure to check with your vet as to what they recommend as treatments change over time.

Causes: exposure to infested pets, spending time outside
Symptoms: itching, bald spots, bleeding
Treatment: prescription medication; Revolution in the US, Stronghold or Ivermectin in the UK

2) Preventing Illness in Holland Lop Rabbits

There are several things you can do to help protect your rabbit against disease. The most important thing is to provide your rabbit with a clean, healthy environment. It is essential that you clean your rabbit's cage on a regular basis and provide plenty of fresh water for him to drink. You should also be sure to provide a healthy, varied diet that meets all of your rabbit's nutritional needs.

In addition to these basic precautions, it is also wise to take your rabbit in for yearly exams and to keep him up to date on all of the recommended vaccinations. Two of the most important vaccines for rabbits are against myxomatosis and rabbit hemorrhagic disease (RHD). These vaccines are available as single vaccines, which need to be taken nine days apart every six months, or as a single combined vaccine once a year.

It is a good idea to have your rabbit examined by a vet as soon as possible after you bring it home. Your vet will be able to assess your rabbit's condition and set a schedule for future check-ups. Additionally, your vet will also offer recommendations on what vaccines your rabbit needs and how often he needs them. It may seem like a needless cost to take your rabbit to the vet once a year but it can save you a lot of money and heartache in diagnosing serious diseases before they become untreatable.

3) Ears, Eyes, Nails and Teeth

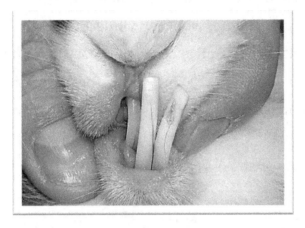

In some rabbits, the teeth are not properly aligned,
a condition called malocclusion.

In addition to vaccinating your rabbit you should also check
its condition on your own from time to time. Take a look
inside your rabbit's ears for signs of wax buildup or
infection – unpleasant odor may also be a sign of infection.
Your rabbit's feet should be dry and free from sores. If you
notice patches of skin where the fur has worn away or
swelling, you should seek immediate veterinary care.
When petting your rabbit, take the time to check its skin
and coat. If you notice white flakes or tiny white dots, your
rabbit could have mites or fleas.

If your rabbit's teeth are not properly aligned they can develop a condition called malocclusion. There are three main causes of this, the most common being genetic predisposition, injury, or bacterial infection. If you provide your rabbit with adequate chew toys, you shouldn't have to worry about its teeth becoming overgrown. You should, however, make frequent checks to see if the teeth are properly aligned – if they aren't, your rabbit could develop molar spurs or abscesses in the mouth.

A rabbit's nails grow continuously so you will need to trim them every six to eight weeks. Trimming your rabbit's nails is not a difficult task but it does require a degree of caution. Inside your rabbit's nail lies the quick – a vein which supplies blood to the nail. If you cut your rabbit's nails too short, you could sever the quick and induce severe bleeding. When clipping your rabbit's nails it is best to only cut off the pointed tip. To be safe, have your veterinarian show you how to properly trim a rabbit's nails before you try it yourself.

One of the most common causes of runny eyes in rabbits is a bacterial eye infection. These infections can be very dangerous and must be treated by a veterinarian as soon as possible. In many cases, antibiotics will be prescribed to handle the infection.

Obstructions and inflammation in the eye may be the result of natural or unnatural causes. In some cases, a piece of bedding or some other object may get stuck in the eye causing it to water or become inflamed. It is also possible, however, for a misshapen eyelid or part of the bone in the rabbit's face to cause an obstruction. If the flow of tears is obstructed, they may form a path down the cheek, discoloring the fur. Depending on the cause of the obstruction, surgery may be necessary to correct the issue.

If the rabbit's eyes do not produce enough tears on their own, they may become dry and irritated. When the eyes become too dry, they are more prone to scratches and erosions which can have a devastating effect on your rabbit's ability to see properly. Some of the symptoms of dry eyes include squinting, eye discharge, redness and inflammation. Trauma to the eye can also interfere with the production of tears and should be evaluated by a veterinarian.

Depending what type of litter you use in your rabbit's cage, your rabbit could develop water eyes as a result of allergies. Dust from the litter, hay or food in your rabbit's cage can get into the eyes and cause irritation. To prevent this from happening, choose litter that is dust-free and make sure the cage is well ventilated.

Chapter Seven: Breeding Holland Lop Rabbits

The following is intended as a broad overview only. If you decide to move forward with the breeding of rabbits, you will need to conduct extensive research in the process and make sure that you have all the necessary supplies on hands. Little lives will be depending on you!

Holland Lop Rabbits are very prolific breeders – a single doe is capable of producing a litter of kits every 30 days. While your rabbits are most certainly going to breed if you simply keep a male and a female together, this may not be the best strategy. If you plan to breed your rabbits you need to follow some precautions and make some preparations in order to ensure the health and well-being of your rabbits and their kits.

1) Basic Breeding Information

You've already learned that a female Holland Lop Rabbit is called a doe and a male is called a buck. When a male and female rabbit are mated, the female may become pregnant with a litter of kits. Young females typically give birth to only 1 or 2 kits in their first birth. Subsequent litters, however, may contain 2 to 4 kits on average. During early breeding sessions, it is not uncommon for a doe to give birth to one or more stillborn kits.

After mating and conception, the doe enters what is called a gestation period. The gestation period is simply the length of time it takes for the kits to develop inside the dam's womb. In Holland Lop Rabbits, the gestation period typically lasts about 30 days. During the final 2 weeks of the pregnancy, it is important that you provide the doe with a high-protein diet to support the development of the kits and milk production. Your vet can help advise you on this if you are not used to the process.

2) The Breeding Process

Before you introduce your male and female rabbits to each other, you need to be sure they are both healthy and of good breeding age. Holland Lop Rabbits tend to prefer breeding in the morning and evening, so these are the best times to attempt a mating. Ideally, the female rabbit should be brought into the male rabbit's cage rather than the other way around. If you put the male in the female's cage, he may be too distracted by the strange environment to mate.

It is not uncommon for the female rabbit to spend a few minutes exploring the cage after being introduced. Once she is ready for mating, she will stretch herself out and raise her tail. It should not take long for the male to climb on and the mating process itself takes only a few seconds.

You do not need to remove the female rabbit immediately – wait a few minutes to see if they breed again. Multiple couplings can increase the chance of pregnancy and may also increase the size of the litter. You will know when the doe is ready to leave because she will refuse the buck's advances – she may even turn and attack him.

After breeding, Holland Lop does often become a little moody. Due to her unpredictable behavior during this time, it is best to keep her isolated. The gestation period lasts about 30 days and it is best to set up a nest box in the cage after 26 days or so. The female rabbit will line the nest box with hay in preparation for kindling and may also pull out some of her own fur to line the nest.

Once the birthing process begins, it typically only takes 20 minutes. Holland Lop Rabbits generally have litters of 2 to 4 kits, though new mothers may have fewer. The doe may wait a few hours after birth to feed the kits, so do not be alarmed. You should check the babies after birth and remove any stillborn kits. After that, leave the babies alone for at least the first day so as not to agitate the mother.

3) Raising the Babies

Once the babies have been born, the doe will do all of the work caring for her kits. The most important aspect in caring for newborn kits is to make sure they stay warm. Sometimes new mothers will give birth to their kits outside the nest box – it is essential that you move them carefully to the nest box so they stay warm. After doing so, do not touch or move the babies for at least a day or two.

Heat lamps with thermostats are available in a price range of $35-$50 / £22.75-£32.50 with replacement bulbs averaging $10-$15 / £6.50-£9.75. Do monitor them carefully though.

In most cases, the dam will start feeding her babies after a few hours. Do not be worried if you don't see her feeding the kits because baby rabbits only need to feed for a few minutes each day. Generally, feedings are done in the early morning or evening when you may not be around anyway. In case you don't see the babies feeding, check the shape of their bodies to see if they are being fed. Well-fed babies should have rounded bellies that puff out to the sides.

When the baby rabbits are first born they will be blind, deaf and hairless. After a day or two, they will begin to develop a layer of fuzz which will help keep them warm. After 1 ½ weeks, the kits should open their eyes and their ears should come up as well. Do not be worried if the ears do not appear to be lopped – it can take several months (or even years) for this to happen. After about 3 weeks, the babies generally start to sample solid food and they should be completely weaned around 5 weeks of age.

Once the kits are weaned it is best to remove the mother from the cage. You can continue to keep the kits together for another few weeks but separate them when they reach 2 months old. Though most Holland Lops do not become sexually mature until 3 or 4 months of age, some do sooner.

Young bucks may also start fighting at which point it is recommended that you separate them.

a) Summary of Breeding Facts:

Sexually Mature (Doe): 3 to 4 months average

Sexually Mature (Buck): 4 to 5 months average

Breeding Age: 6 months

Litter Size: 1 to 2 (first breeding); 2 to 4 average

Gestation Period: lasts about 30 days

Birthing Process: 20 minutes average

Eyes and Ears Open: 1 ½ weeks

Solid Food: begin sampling around 3 weeks

Weaning: around 5 weeks

Chapter Eight: Showing Holland Lop Rabbits

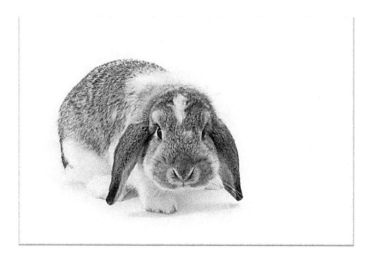

1) Breed Standard

The breed standard as set forth by the American Rabbit Breeders Association (ARBA) designates 84 points for general type, 7 points for fur and 9 points for other characteristics. A breakdown of the standard of points is as follows:

General Type – 84 points
Body (32 points)
Head (24 points)
Ears (10 points)

Crown (8 points)

Feet, Legs and Bone (10 points)

Fur – 7 points

Color/Markings – 4 points

Condition – 5 points

<u>Total Points = 100 points possible</u>

The British Rabbit Council (BRC), which recognizes the Holland Lop as the Miniature Lop, divides the points differently. A breakdown of the BRC's point system for the Miniature Lop standard is as follows:

Type – 30 points

Coat – 20 points

Ears – 30 points

Color and Pattern – 15 points

Condition – 5 points

<u>Total Points = 100 points possible</u>

2) What to Know Before Showing

Before you attempt to show your Holland Lop Rabbit you should be very familiar with the breed standard to be sure your rabbit qualifies. Both the ARBA and the BRC provide complete copies of the breed standard on their websites that you can peruse.

Below you will find several key things to look for when assessing your rabbit's qualifications for show:

Type = thickset and firm; short and broad body with a muscled neck
- Rump is short and rounded
- Front lets are short and thick
- Hind legs are short and strong
- Small dewlap is allowed, but not desirable

Weight = ideal weight is 3.5 lbs. (1.5 kg), maximum is 3.8 lbs. (1.6 kg)

Coat = dense and of good length; abundance of guard hairs
- Legs and pads should be well furred
- Head is bold and broad
- Eyes are large and bright

- Basal ridge is prominent, forms a crown across the top of the skull
- Ears are thick and broad - rounded at the ends

Color and Pattern = all colors and patterns accepted except broken pattern

Condition = perfect state of health
- Free from soiling on all body parts
- Coat reflects good overall health

Faults (loss of points)

- Body too long
- Head not properly characteristic of breed
- Ears are damaged or pimpled
- Light soiling on the feet, ears and genitals
- Fur is slightly soiled or matted
- Toenails too long
- Rear feet are not parallel to body

Disqualifications

- Mutilated or maloccluded teeth
- Over weight limit
- Feet are bowed or bent
- Crooked tail
- Any discernible disease or illness
- Full or partial blindness
- Matted coat

3) Packing for a Show

The key to success in rabbit shows is to be prepared. This involves making sure your rabbit meets the breed standard and arranging the rabbit properly for judging. There are further details available from a range of websites at the back of the book which should prove helpful.

However, you should also prepare yourself by bringing along an emergency kit, just in case.

Included in your emergency kit should be:

- Nail clippers – for emergency nail trimming
- Antibiotic ointment
- Band-Aids – for minor injuries to self, not rabbit
- Hydrogen peroxide – for cleaning injuries and spots on white coats
- Slicker brush – to smooth rough coats
- Black felt-tip pen
- Business cards
- Paper towels – because you never know
- Scrap carpet square – for last-minute grooming
- Collapsible stool – when chairs are not available
- Extra clothes
- Supplies for your rabbits

Chapter Nine: Holland Lop Rabbits Care Sheet

1) Basic Information

Scientific Name: *Oryctolagus cuniculus*

Size: up to 4 lbs. (1.8 kg)

Coloration: any color or pattern is acceptable

Build: small and compact

Ears: lopped (pendulous rather than erect)

Lifespan: 7 to 9 years

Diet: herbivorous

Foods: commercial rabbit pellets, Timothy hay, vegetables and fruits

Supplements: generally not required if the diet is sufficient in fiber and protein but can be added to their drink

2) Cage Set-up Guide

Location Options: indoor vs. outdoor

Cage Types: single-level, multi-level, open pen

Cage Materials: metal cage with wire mesh sides, solid bottom

Bedding: non-toxic pellets, fresh hay, newspaper

Accessories: water bottle, food bowls, hay compartment, litter pan, chew toys, shelter

3) Feeding Guide

Diet Basics: low protein, high fiber

Main Diet: high-quality alfalfa pellets

Nutritional Breakdown: 16% or less protein, 20% to 25% fiber

Ingredients to Avoid: corn, binders, feed dust

Supplemental Foods: Timothy hay, fresh fruits, fresh vegetables

Amount to Feed: 1 oz. pellets per pound bodyweight, unlimited hay, and small portion of fruit/vegetable daily

Other Needs: unlimited supply of fresh water

4) Breeding Information

Sexually Mature (Doe): 3 to 4 months average

Sexually Mature (Buck): 4 to 5 months average

Breeding Age: 6 months

Litter Size: 1 to 2 (first breeding); 2 to 4 average

Gestation Period: lasts about 30 days

Birthing Process: 20 minutes average

Eyes and Ears Open: 1 ½ weeks

Solid Food: begin sampling around 3 weeks

Weaning: around 5 weeks

5) General Rabbit Care Tips

a) Holding Your Rabbit

It is important to remember that Holland Lop Rabbits are fragile creatures so you need to use caution when handling them. The first thing you need to know is that you must never pick up your rabbit by the ears. When you first bring your rabbit home you should give it a day or two to get used to the new environment before you try to hold it.

When you feel your rabbit is ready, offer it a few treats to encourage the rabbit to approach you on its own. Once your rabbit approaches you, begin petting it gently on the back and ears. If your rabbit responds well to this treatment you can try picking it up. Make sure to support your rabbit's feet and hold the rabbit's body against your chest. Do not let children handle the rabbit and be careful when putting it back down.

b) Introducing Your Rabbit to Children

Holland Lop Rabbits are a very gentle breed so they have the capacity to get along with children. If your children are not properly educated in how to handle the rabbit, however, it could result in accidental injury. Before you bring your rabbit home, make sure to talk to your children about the responsibilities of their new pet. Teach your children how to properly hold the rabbit and warn them that the rabbit might be frightened by loud noises.

Once you bring your rabbit home, give it time to acclimate to its new surroundings. After your rabbit has become comfortable at home you can try introducing it to your children. Hold the rabbit securely in your arms and let your child pet it gently. If your rabbit is calm, you can try setting it down on the ground so your child can pet it. Do not let your children pick the rabbit up unless they are old enough to know how to do so properly.

c) Shedding in Rabbits

Some rabbits shed more than others but most breeds shed every three months. Like cats, rabbits are very clean animals and they like to groom themselves. Unlike cats, however, rabbits cannot vomit – thus, if they consume too much hair it could form a ball in the stomach and cause serious health problems.

For this reason, it is essential that you brush your rabbit at least once a week to remove loose and dead hairs from its coat. During shedding seasons, you may need to brush Holland Lop Rabbits once a day or even multiple times a day to keep up.

Chapter Ten: Myths and Misconceptions

Not everything you read on the internet is true. You probably already know this, but many inexperienced rabbit owners make mistakes with their rabbits based on improper information found on the internet. In order to provide your rabbit with the best care possible, you should familiarize yourself with some of the myths and misconceptions that exist regarding rabbit care. Once you know the basics you will be able to differentiate between fact and myth and raise your rabbit the right way.

1) Myths and Misconceptions

You Should Never Feed Your Rabbit Grass
– FALSE

There is a common myth that feeding your rabbit grass will cause bloat and/or diarrhea. In reality, grass can actually be good for your rabbit! After all, wild rabbits eat a diet that consists primarily of grass, right? You do, however, need to be careful about letting your rabbit munch on the grass in your yard. If you use fertilizers, pesticides or other chemical lawn treatments it could be dangerous for your rabbit. As an alternative, try growing a pot or container of grass for your rabbit indoors.

You Should Never Feed Your Rabbit Fruit
– FALSE

This myth is founded on the idea that feeding rabbit fruit or other sweet foods encourages the growth of bacteria. While refined sugars are most certainly not ideal for rabbits to eat, natural sugars (fructose) like those found in fruit are perfectly okay but be careful of the quantities given. In fact, grass and hay naturally contain some of this sugar anyway.

Rabbits Need to be Kept in Pairs
– FALSE

If you perform some basic research on keeping rabbits as pets you are likely to find a number of resources claiming that rabbits need to be kept in pairs or they might become "lonely". Keep in mind that "lonely" is a human emotion – rabbits do not have human feelings. As long as you provide your rabbit with plenty of attention and human interaction, it will be perfectly fine on its own.

Rabbits Don't Need to go to the Vet
– FALSE

While rabbits may not require a routine vaccination schedule like dogs and cats in the US, it is recommended in the UK for Myxomatosis and Viral Haemorrhagic Disease (VHD). It is also often required for getting pet insurance, holiday boarding and attending events. After reading the health section of this book you should know that many rabbit diseases progress rapidly, often without showing any symptoms. This being the case, taking your rabbit to the vet once or twice a year may be the only way to catch diseases before they progress beyond recovery.

Pet Rabbits Best Kept Outdoors
– FALSE

There are benefits to keeping a rabbit outdoors but you should think carefully before you do so. Some rabbit owners claim that rabbits should ONLY be kept outdoors while others claim that indoors is best. The choice is ultimately yours to make but keep in mind that outdoor rabbits are more likely to be exposed to disease, inclement weather and extreme temperatures. They may also not get as much attention as indoor rabbits which could affect their temperament and overall well-being.

Rabbits Love to be Picked Up
- FALSE

While many rabbit breeds including the Holland Lop are very friendly by nature, they generally do not like being picked up and held. Being held so high off the ground can be frightening for a rabbit, so it is best to enjoy their company on the floor at your rabbit's level.

2) *Common Mistakes*

a) Using the Wrong Bedding

Choosing the right type of bedding is very important for Holland Lop Rabbits -- certain kinds of bedding can get stuck in their coats. For this reason, you should avoid using shavings as bedding. A better option is to use straw or hay. When purchasing bedding, be sure it is non-toxic and fresh – you should also shake off as much dust as possible before using the bedding in your rabbit cage.

b) Feeding the Wrong Food

The food you offer your Holland Lop Rabbits has a direct impact on their health. You probably already understand the importance of eating the right foods for your own health, so it should be easy to see how the same is true of pet rabbits. Rabbits are herbivores by nature which means they receive all their daily nutrition from plant based foods.

The main component of a Holland Lop Rabbit's diet should be grass hay like Timothy or meadow hay. You can also supplement your rabbit's diet with legume hay, fresh vegetables and commercial rabbit pellets. Do not assume that if you only give your rabbit commercial pellets he will be healthy – these pellets are not enough to give your rabbit the nutrition he requires.

Some rabbit owners also make the mistake of making changes in their rabbit's diet too quickly. Rabbits have very delicate digestive systems so any changes to their diets must be made slowly. Juvenile rabbits should not be fed vegetables while their digestive systems are still developing. Once they reach maturity, however, you can slowly begin introducing vegetables and then may offer them a variety of vegetables on a daily basis.

c) Unwanted Breeding

Inexperienced rabbit owners sometimes fail to understand just how quickly and how often rabbits are capable of breeding. A female rabbit's estrus (heat) cycle is so frequent that she is almost continuously capable of getting pregnant. This is an important fact to keep in mind when keeping male and female rabbits in the same cage.

Many rabbit owners encounter unwanted breeding when they fail to separate the sexes early enough. Though female rabbits reach sexual maturity around 3 to 4 months of age and males around 5 to 6 months, they are capable of breeding as early as 2 or 3 months. To avoid unwanted breeding, it is essential that you separate the sexes before that point.

This is most likely to happen after a new litter is born. If you do not have experience keeping or breeding rabbits, you may not expect rabbits from the same litter to breed so readily. If you allow rabbits from the same litter to breed it can result in inbreeding and genetic defects. You shouldn't even keep male and female rabbits in the same cage outside a period of time long enough for them to mate, after which point the female should be removed from the cage.

Chapter Eleven: Relevant Websites

1) Shopping

When you start looking around the internet it can take some time to track down exactly what you are looking for.

A one-stop shop for all your rabbit needs is what is required and the sites below offer you the convenience of pulling together many of the best products from around the web.

Enjoy Shopping!

United States Website
www.rabbitsorbunnies.com

United Kingdom Website
www.rabbitsorbunnies.co.uk

2) *Food for Holland Lop Rabbits*

United States Websites:

"Holland Lop Diet." Holland Lop Rabbits.
hollandloprabbits.blogspot.com/2011/02/holland-lop-diet.html

"Holland Lop Care Information." Double S Rabbitry.
www.freewebs.com/doublesrabbitry/hollandlopcareinfo.htm

"Feeding Your Rabbit." Three Little Ladies Rabbitry.
www.threelittleladiesrabbitry.com/feeding.php

Hess, Sylvia. "Alfalfa Pellets are not Equal." Holland Lop Rabbit Specialty Club. www.hlrsc.com/

United Kingdom Websites:

"Feeding Rabbits." Provet Health Care.
www.provet.co.uk/rabbits/rabbitfeeding.htm

"Rabbit Diet Myths." The Royal Society for the Prevention of Cruelty to Animals.
www.rspca.org.uk/allaboutanimals/pets/rabbits/diet/myths

"Diets." PDSA.org.uk.
www.pdsa.org.uk/pet-health-advice/rabbits/diet

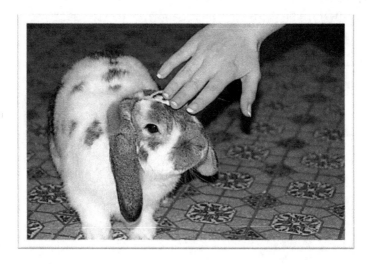

3) Care for Holland Lop Rabbits

United States Websites:

"Basic Holland Care." Hillsboro Hollands.
www.hillsborohollands.com/Holland_Lop_Care.html

"Holland Care." Utah Holland Lops.
www.utahhollandlops.com/hollandcaresheet.htm

"Holland Lop." Gio's Holland Lops.
www.gioshollandlops.com/a-thing-about-hollands.html

United Kingdom Websites:

"Miniature Lop." The British Rabbit Council.
www.thebrc.org/standards/L8-Lop%20Miniature.pdf

"Miniature Lop Profile." Mini Rabbit Ranch.
www.minirabbitranch.co.uk/miniaturelopprofile.htm

"Bunny Care." Dee Millen Rabbits.
www.miniloprabbit.co.uk/5.html

4) *Health Information for Holland Lop Rabbits*

United States Websites:

"Pet Rabbit Health." My House Rabbit.
www.myhouserabbit.com/health.php

"Rabbits as Pets: Guide to a Happy Healthy Rabbit."
Animal-World. animal-
world.com/encyclo/critters/rabbits/RabbitProfile.htm

"Rabbit Health." House Rabbit Society.
rabbit.org/category/health/

United Kingdom Websites:

Millen, Dee. "Vaccinations and Health Care." Dee Millen
Rabbits.
www.deemillen.co.uk/bunny_care_and_housing.php#healt
h

"Benefits of Neutering." AdorableRabbits.co.uk.
www.adorablerabbits.co.uk/neutering.htm

"Health." PDSA.org.uk.
www.pdsa.org.uk/pet-health-advice/rabbits/health

5) Breeding Information for Holland Lop Rabbits

United States Websites:

"Tips for Breeders." The Wonderful World of Pet Rabbits. www.petrabbitworld.com/helpful_tips.html

"Rabbit Breeding." Snowberry. www.snow-berry.com/breeding.htm

"Holland Lop Rabbit Breeders." RabbitBreeders.us. rabbitbreeders.us/holland-lop-rabbit-breeders

Andrews, T.L. "Breeding: How To." Holland Lop Rabbit Specialty Club. www.hlrsc.com/

United Kingdom Websites:

"Company." PDSA.org.uk. www.pdsa.org.uk/pet-health-advice/rabbits/company

"Do I Really Want to or Need to Breed my Rabbit." Rabbit Rehome. www.rabbitrehome.org.uk/care/breedingrabbits.asp

"Breeding Rabbits." CaringBear.co.uk. www.caringbear.co.uk/rabbits/breeding/

6) Showing Holland Lop Rabbits

United States Websites:

"Showing and Judging." Holland Lop Rabbit Specialty Club. www.hlrsc.com/

"The Basics of Showing Rabbits." Three Little Ladies Rabbitry.
www.threelittleladiesrabbitry.com/showingindex.php

"Holland Lop Breed Standard." Oak Ridge Rabbitry.
oakridgerabbitry.weebly.com/holland-lop-type.html

United Kingdom Websites:

"Miniature Lop Standard." The National Miniature Lop Rabbit Club. www.nmlrc.co.uk/standard.htm

"Showing Rabbits." Springfield Rabbits.
www.springfieldrabbits.co.uk/showingrabbits.htm

"BRC Mini Lop Standard." JJ's Lops.
www.jjs-lops.co.uk/brc-mini-lop-standard.htm

Index:

clean up · 62

cleaning · 34, 99

clipping · 83

color · 3, 8, 19, 20, 21, 100

colors · 6, 7, 11, 19, 22, 96

conception · 87

costs · 33, 34, 35, 36

D

death · 65, 69, 78

dental problems · 76

dermatophytosisis · 70

diarrhea · 71, 72, 73, 107

diet · 54, 55, 63, 73, 80, 87, 100, 107, 111

disease · 25, 40, 43, 45, 49, 65, 66, 67, 69, 71, 72, 73, 74, 75, 78, 80, 81, 97, 109

doe · 10, 11, 18, 86, 87, 89, 90

does · 18, 23, 24, 46, 69, 71, 89

dogs · 29, 30, 108

E

ears · 1, 3, 4, 5, 11, 14, 15, 20, 21, 30, 45, 75, 79, 91, 97

enterotoxemia · 73

exercise · 46, 47, 50

F

federal law · 24

feed · 35, 54, 55, 56, 57, 59, 60, 89, 91, 101

female rabbit · 3, 18, 78, 87, 88, 89, 112

fiber · 55, 56, 73, 76, 100, 101

fleas · 79

food · 4, 16, 31, 33, 35, 52, 55, 56, 57, 58, 59, 66, 91, 101, 111

food bowl · 33, 53

fruits · 57, 100, 101
fur · 6, 12, 74, 79, 89, 93, 94, 97

G

gestation period · 87, 89, 92, 102
grass · 50, 107, 111
grooming supplies · 34

H

habitat · 46
hairballs · 56
handling · 42, 103
hay · 35, 48, 54, 56, 58, 60, 62, 89, 100, 101, 107, 110, 111
head tilt · 68, 77
health · 27, 39, 44, 45, 54, 58, 63, 64, 87, 96, 108, 111
healthy · 2, 39, 43, 44, 45, 58, 63, 80, 88, 111
history · 1, 2, 9, 12, 13, 45, 136
Holland Lop Specialty Club · 40
human interaction · 45, 50, 108
hutch · 33, 35

I

inbreeding · 112
indoors · 46, 48, 51, 107, 109
infection · 67, 68, 70
initial costs · 31, 32, 34, 35

K

kindling · 4, 89
kits · 3, 4, 10, 11, 14, 15, 16, 18, 44, 86, 87, 89, 90, 91

other pets · 29, 30, 37, 79
otitis media · 68
outdoors · 46, 47, 48, 51, 53, 109

P

parasites · 49, 50, 77
patterns · 7, 19, 21, 96
pellets · 54, 55, 56, 57, 58, 59, 60, 100, 101
permit · 23, 24, 25
pets · 1, 5, 6, 9, 23, 29, 30, 37, 50, 63, 79, 108, 115, 117, 137
pregnant · 18, 69, 71, 87, 112
pros and cons · 37, 48
protein · 55, 87, 100, 101
purchase price · 31, 32, 34

Q

Queensland · 25

R

rabbit breeds · 12, 13, 109
rabbit food · 35
rabbit pellets · 35, 55, 56, 100, 111
rabbit run · 47, 53
rabbit shows · 13, 98
ringworm · 70

S

sexual maturity · 16, 17, 18, 112
shedding · 105
shopping · 113

show · 5, 13, 19, 21, 32, 67, 95
spayed or neutered · 24, 31, 32, 34, 78
stillborn kits · 18, 87, 89
stress · 27, 43, 69, 73
supplements · 56, 100, 101, 111
symptoms · 65, 66, 67, 68, 69, 70, 71, 72, 73, 74, 75, 76, 77, 78, 79, 108

T

teeth · 38, 45, 76, 97
temperament · 5, 28, 29, 109
The American Rabbit Breeders' Association · 13
Timothy · 54, 56, 58, 59, 60, 100, 101, 111
travel carrier · 33
treatment · 42, 63, 65, 66, 67, 68, 69, 70, 71, 72, 73, 74, 75, 76, 77, 78, 79
treats · 36, 57, 58, 103
two rabbits · 26, 27, 34, 36

U

uterine cancer · 78

V

vaccinations · 31, 33, 40, 81
vegetables · 35, 54, 57, 58, 100, 101, 111
vet · 33, 36, 81
veterinary care · 31, 33, 35, 36
viral hemorrhagic disease · 66

W

water · 80
water bottle · 16, 33, 101

Photo Credits

Cover Design:- Liliana Gonzalez Garcia, ipublicidades.com (info@ipublicidades.com)

Title Page Photo, By Claire madridspain at en.wikipedia. Later version(s) were uploaded by Morn at en.wikipedia. (Transferred from en.wikipedia) [Public domain], from Wikimedia Commons http://commons.wikimedia.org/wiki/File:Holland_Lop_wit h_Broken_Orange_Coloring.jpg

Page 1 Photo, By Orlandkurtenbach (Own work) [Public domain], via Wikimedia Commons, http://commons.wikimedia.org/wiki/File:Holland_lop_bun ny.JPG

Page 5 Photo, By Maggi, via Wikimedia Commons, http://commons.wikimedia.org/wiki/File:Bl%C3%A5dvv.jpg

Page 7 Photo, By Flickr user Bunnygoth, http://www.flickr.com/photos/bunnygoth/7936036228/sizes/ l/in/photostream/

Page 9 Photo, By Miniaturelop (Own work) [CC-BY-SA-3.0 (http://creativecommons.org/licenses/by-sa/3.0)], via Wikimedia Commons, http://commons.wikimedia.org/wiki/File:Miniature_Lop_-_Front_View.jpg

Page 10 Photo, By Flickr user Matsubokkuri, http://www.flickr.com/photos/matsubokkuri/3116974301/sizes/l/in/photostream/

Page 14 Photo, By Bdk, via Wikimedia Commons, http://commons.wikimedia.org/wiki/File:Baby_rabbit_nest.jpg

Page 15 Photo, By Michelle Skindzelewski (Own work) [Public domain], via Wikimedia Commons, http://commons.wikimedia.org/wiki/File:Born_dec_52008_bunnies_027.JPG

Page 17 Photo, By Miniaturelop via Wikimedia Commons, http://commons.wikimedia.org/wiki/File:Miniature_Lop_-_Grey.jpg

Page 19 Photo, By Mallowtek (Own work) [CC-BY-SA-3.0 (http://creativecommons.org/licenses/by-sa/3.0)], via Wikimedia Commons, http://commons.wikimedia.org/wiki/File:Lapin_nain_b%C3%A9lier_(face).JPG

Page 23 Photo, By Orlandkurtenbach (Own work) [Public domain], via Wikimedia Commons, http://commons.wikimedia.org/wiki/File:Holland_lop.JPG

Page 26 Photo, By Radosław Drożdżewski (Zwiadowca21) (Own work) [CC-BY-SA-3.0 (http://creativecommons.org/licenses/by-sa/3.0)], via Wikimedia Commons, https://commons.wikimedia.org/wiki/File:Deutsche_Widder.JPG

Page 29 Photo, By Flickr user Valeehill, http://www.flickr.com/photos/valeehill/5448471675/sizes/l/in/photostream/

Page 39 Photo, by Josse95, via Wikimedia Commons, http://commons.wikimedia.org/wiki/File:Dv%C3%A4rgv%C3%A4durskanin.jpeg

Page 43 Photo, By Amanda Warren (originally posted to Flickr as So shy) [CC-BY-2.0 (http://creativecommons.org/licenses/by/2.0)], via Wikimedia Commons, http://commons.wikimedia.org/wiki/File:So_shy_Mini_Lop.jpg

Page 46 Photo, By Vera Buhl (Own work) [CC-BY-SA-3.0 (http://creativecommons.org/licenses/by-sa/3.0) or GFDL (http://www.gnu.org/copyleft/fdl.html)], via Wikimedia Commons, http://commons.wikimedia.org/wiki/File:2008-01-24_(8)_Rabbit,_Zwergkaninchen.JPG

Page 51 Photo, By Flickr user Cameron.Small, http://www.flickr.com/photos/57477464@N07/5943591906/sizes/l/in/photostream/

Page 52 Photo, By Flickr user Valeehill, http://www.flickr.com/photos/valeehill/5449081954/sizes/l/in/photostream/

Page 54 Photo, By Luvlopsrabbitry (Own work) [CC-BY-SA-3.0 (http://creativecommons.org/licenses/by-sa/3.0)], via Wikimedia Commons, http://commons.wikimedia.org/wiki/File:LuvLopsRabbitry_HollandLop_Tort.jpg

Page 55 Photo, By ZoidberdBinky, via Wikimedia Commons, http://commons.wikimedia.org/wiki/File:Hollandloplettuce.jpg

Page 59 Photo, By Flickr user Valeehill, http://www.flickr.com/photos/valeehill/5449081004/sizes/z/in/photostream/

Page 63 Photo, By Stephen J. Biles.Stbiles at en.wikipedia [CC-BY-SA-3.0 (http://creativecommons.org/licenses/by-sa/3.0/), GFDL (http://www.gnu.org/copyleft/fdl.html), CC-BY-SA-3.0 (http://creativecommons.org/licenses/by-sa/3.0/)], from Wikimedia Commons, http://commons.wikimedia.org/wiki/File:Bunny_Blu_Blu.jpg

Page 80 Photo, By Luisa Blor (Own work) [CC-BY-SA-3.0 (http://creativecommons.org/licenses/by-sa/3.0)], via Wikimedia Commons, http://commons.wikimedia.org/wiki/File:Teddy_das_kaninnchen.JPG

Page 82 Photo By Uwe Gille (Own work) http://commons.wikimedia.org/wiki/File:Bradygnathia-superior-rabbit.jpg

Page 96 photo by By Orlandkurtenbach (Own work) [Public domain], via Wikimedia Commons https://commons.wikimedia.org/wiki/File%3AHolland_lop. JPG

Page 98 Photo, By JirjenJirjen at de.wikipedia [GFDL (http://www.gnu.org/copyleft/fdl.html) or CC-BY-SA-3.0 (http://creativecommons.org/licenses/by-sa/3.0/)], from Wikimedia Commons, http://commons.wikimedia.org/wiki/File:Balkonhasen.jpg

Page 100 Photo, By User Axes0728 on sv.wikipedia [GFDL (http://www.gnu.org/copyleft/fdl.html) or CC-BY-SA-3.0 (http://creativecommons.org/licenses/by-sa/3.0/)], via Wikimedia Commons, http://commons.wikimedia.org/wiki/File:Dverg_vedur.jpg

Page 103 Photo, Lucki19 at en.wikipedia [CC-BY-SA-3.0 (http://creativecommons.org/licenses/by-sa/3.0) or GFDL (http://www.gnu.org/copyleft/fdl.html)], from Wikimedia Commons, http://commons.wikimedia.org/wiki/File:Mini_Lop.jpg

Page 106 Photo, By shogun1192 (own pict. shot) [Public domain], via Wikimedia Commons,
http://commons.wikimedia.org/wiki/File:Hollandlopear.JPG

Page 110 Photo, Page 107 Photo, By Franie Frou
http://commons.wikimedia.org/wiki/File:Mini_lop.jpg

Page 113, Image courtesy www.rabbitsorbunnies.com/

Page 115 Photo, By Flickr user Celebdu,
www.flickr.com/photos/celebdu/385234593/sizes/l/in/photostream/

References

"Bacterial and Mycotic Diseases of Rabbits." The Merck Veterinary Manual. www.merckmanuals.com/vet/exotic_and_laboratory_animals/rabbits/bacterial_and_mycotic_diseases_of_rabbits.html

"Birth and Babies." WelshRabbitry.com. www.welshrabbitry.com/birth.html

"Bunny Care and Housing." Dee Millen Rabbits. www.deemillen.co.uk/bunny_care_and_housing.php#health

Carter, Christine. "Rabbit Jargon." *The Wonderful World of Pet Rabbits*. www.petrabbitworld.com/clubs_jargon.html

"Diseases A-Z: Rabbit." PetMD. www.petmd.com/rabbit/conditions#.Uc3iv_lmjZg

"Dwarf Rabbit FAQ – Holland Lop Care Information." The Nature Trail. www.thenaturetrail.com/rabbit-care/dwarf-lop-faq/

"Health Concerns for Your Rabbit." Zooh Corner. www.mybunny.org/info/health.htm

"History of the Holland Lop." D&A Rabbitry.
http://dnarabbitry.tripod.com/history.htm

Holevinski, Jaylene. "Packing for a Rabbit Show." Holland Lop Rabbit Specialty Club.
www.hlrsc.com/Articles/packing.html

"Holland Care." Utah Holland Lops.
www.utahhollandlops.com/hollandcaresheet.htm

"Holland Lop." Gio's Holland Lops.
www.gioshollandlops.com/a-thing-about-hollands.html

"Holland Lop Care Information." Double S. Rabbitry.
www.freewebs.com/doublesrabbitry/hollandlopcareinfo.htm

"Holland Lop Colors." Backyard Bunnies Rabbitry.
http://backyardbunniesrabbitry.webs.com/hollandlopcolors.htm

"Holland Lop Show Standards." Hillsboro Hollands.
www.hillsborohollands.com/Standard.html

"Holland Lops – Standards." Three Little Ladies.
www.threelittleladiesrabbitry.com/hollandlopsstandard.php

"Miniature Lop." The British Rabbit Council.
www.thebrc.org/standards/L8-Lop%20Miniature.pdf

"Myths & Misconceptions." The Wonderful World of Pet
Rabbits. www.petrabbitworld.com/myth_busting.html

"Rabbits as Pets." Animal-World. http://animal-
world.com/encyclo/critters/rabbits/RabbitProfile.htm

"Rabbit Breeding." Snow-Berry.
www.snow-berry.com/breeding.htm

Roquet, Jana. "The 3 P's of Potty Box Training Your
Rabbits." Holland Lop Rabbit Specialty Club.
http://www.hlrsc.com/Articles/pottytraining.html

"Taking Care of Your Precious Hollands." Hillsboro
Hollands.
www.hillsborohollands.com/Holland_Lop_Care.html

"Tips for Breeders." The Wonderful World of Pet Rabbits.
www.petrabbitworld.com/helpful_tips.html

"Viral Diseases of Rabbits." The Merck Veterinary Manual. www.merckmanuals.com/vet/exotic_and_laboratory_animals/rabbits/viral_diseases_of_rabbits.html

"Your Breeding Questions Answered." The Wonderful World of Pet Rabbits. www.petrabbitworld.com/breeding_questions.html

Notes:

CPSIA information can be obtained
at www.ICGtesting.com
Printed in the USA
LVHW050610300420
653803LV00012BA/160